Rural America

A PICTORIAL FOLK MEMORY

Rural America

A PICTORIAL FOLK MEMORY

BY MARY A. SHAFER

WILLOW CREEK PRESS

Minocqua, Wisconsin

Dedication

For my grandmother, Mary B. Wharton, who gave me my own sense of place through the gifts of her love, her stories, and my mother.

ISBN 1-57223-021-5

Published by WILLOW CREEK PRESS, an imprint of Outlook Publishing, P.O. Box 147, Minocqua, WI 54548

For information on other Willow Creek titles, write or call 1-800-850-WILD.

Printed in the U.S.A.

Library of Congress Cataloging-in-Publication Data

Shafer, Mary A.
   Rural America : a pictorial folk memory / by Mary A. Shafer.
      p.   cm.
   ISBN 1-57223-021-5 (alk. paper)
   1. Country life—United States. 2. United States—Social life and customs. 3. United States—Pictorial works. 4. United States—Description and travel.   I. Title.
E161.S45   1995
973'.09734—dc20
                                                    95–17767
                                                    CIP

CONTENTS

ACKNOWLEDGMENTS

No creative work is a solitary effort, and I would like to thank several people for their help in making this book possible.

First of all, I'd like to thank Tom Petrie for giving me the opportunity to write it, and for being a generous, understanding, and very pleasant publisher to work with. The process of producing a book is a long one that presents many challenges, but this project went as smoothly as could be hoped, thanks to the very dedicated publishing professionals at Willow Creek Press. Their concern for quality and their efforts to make this the best book it could possibly be are greatly appreciated.

Thanks to Greg Linder, whose literary finesse gave my words polish and readability, and whose friendship and professional skills are most valued. I am grateful also to Pat Linder for a fine design job on this material, and for her sense of detail.

Mrs. Thelma Olson Bryan was most generous in allowing me to use excerpts from her mother Elisabeth's memoirs of growing up on the midwestern frontier, and she was a delight to talk with. Her enthusiasm for this project was infectious and renewed my own interest in things genealogical.

I am grateful to my friend Lucinda "Goo" Gohman and her father, Richard, for making me aware of Mrs. Olson's story, which is included in a family history that Mr. Gohman is currently putting together. His project reminded me that it is the "story" in "history" that is so fascinating.

Steve Daily was very helpful to my photo research efforts at the Milwaukee County Historical Society, and his patience with my many requests is appreciated.

Dr. Dan Magnussen, a former professor of mine who is largely responsible for awakening the latent historian in me, was kind enough to review my manuscript, make suggestions, and write the foreword for this book. His incredible grasp of history and his vast factual knowledge are a constant source of amazement and usefulness to me, but I value most his friendship, straightforwardness, and interest.

Of course, my family has been a constant source of support and inspiration for all my work, and I am thankful for their love and belief in me.

Most of all I would like to thank my partner, Sharon Mahos, for her understanding during long stretches of work that meant I neglected the everyday things, and for giving me the space and time I needed to complete my research and writing. Anyone who has ever written a book, composed a piece of music, undertaken a painting, or engaged in any other creative endeavor knows that a stalwart companion is indispensable to the health of the muse.

This barefoot young woman pauses in her field labors, perhaps reflecting on the beautifully tailored dresses she might have worn if she had been born a gentlewoman. But practicality reigned supreme in a harsh land, and she was probably thankful for the protection from sun and mosquitoes afforded by her straw hat and head rag. 🖋

LIFE IN
HURST, L.I.

Hand-Col.

FOREWORD

This beautifully written work by Mary A. Shafer is something that has been needed to fill a gap created by a lack of writers concerning themselves with the original backbone of America—the country people, from the pioneers to the modern-day farmers. *Rural America: A Pictorial Folk Memory* is a nostalgic journey through a crucial period in our history, beginning with the nineteenth century and proceeding into the twentieth.

If hard work is necessary for success, this book is about people who performed that work and how they did it. It is about people who wrenched a living from the land while developing a reverence for the soil they tilled. They, no doubt, never thought much about it, but they also provided the food that the non-country people would come to rely upon for daily sustenance.

This book will bring back a flood of memories for many readers who once lived on or visited country farms. It is a way of life that has been disappearing of late, but it is Americana at its best, and we all should remember that.

Daniel O. Magnussen
Emeritus Professor of History
Lacey, Washington, 1995

INTRODUCTION

At its heart, this book is a question, and surrounding it are the vestiges of my search for its answer. If life is a journey and not a destination, then perhaps this question has a pertinence today that is even more urgent than in times past.

My world, as I know it, spins at an almost impossible pace, even for someone who was raised in the age of space flight, fax machines, and laser surgery. The future looks as incomprehensible to me as my world would have appeared to my great grandmother. Yet time spirals endlessly onward, and we are swept along, ready or not. I passionately believe that we cannot know where we are going until we fully understand where we have been, and that the only way we can anticipate what's ahead is by occasionally looking back.

We need not look back sadly, as if lamenting our losses, although that's certainly part of it; on the other hand, the review should not become some boastful recounting of what we perceive to be our gains. Mostly, I think, we benefit by digging away at the accumulated debris of time's passage that enshrouds what really matters—the visions that spurred our ancestors to feats of courage and shame, greatness and folly, glory and defeat. When we relive and honestly feel the passion of these visions, we can come to some measure of understanding and appreciation of our forebears' role in the collective journey and, by extrapolation, our own role.

We don't arrive at this comprehension by studying such isolated and overwrought events as presidential elections and wars. These phenomena, it seems to me, are too falsely intense and parochial to be used as measures of our true nature as a society. I believe that coming to some understanding of ourselves as countrymen won't happen only by examining how we govern, fight, or die; it's also essential to ponder how it is that we choose to live.

It would be presumptious of me, as a young woman living in the 1990s, to claim to know what life was like when America was still basically a rural, agrarian nation. I can know what I've been told by those few who

still remember what it was like to grow up before the automobile, the telephone, and the airplane made the world a smaller, faster place. And I can understand, through stories and some of my own experiences, what it took to grow one's own food, keep a wood fire lit in the furnace, and sit through a long winter's night with only the light from a kerosene-soaked wick to illuminate the page of a book.

Yet I can only imagine what it meant to *have* to do these things, day in and day out. I can only guess at the depth of the motivations that led young people—and some who were not so young—to commit themselves to the hardships of a rural life; to settle a hard land and then to stay.

I recorded here the musings of a curious mind, a cerebral reaching for some bridge between who we once were and who we have become as a nation, viewed in the context of a way of life that is as old as the country itself. Interspersed with my words is a collection of fascinating photographs that bring closer to home some of the images that passed through my mind as I wrote. I truly hope you enjoy both elements, and that you find the time you spend with this book worthwhile, if only to allow yourself the kind of meditation and mental "breathing space" that it celebrates.

Mary A. Shafer
Milwaukee, Wisconsin
March, 1995

CHAPTER 1

DOWN COUNTRY ROADS

Down Country Roads

The Country.

The phrase is always uttered with a hint of reverence, spoken in such a way that you know the words begin with capital letters. The two simple little words carry on their backs a thousand and more years of what remains indelibly inscribed in our collective psyche to this day: a kinship with those things not of our own making, not under our control, and just beyond the fringe of what we have come to think of as civilized. These humble words are imbued with the power of everything we have failed to master: the wind and all that rides upon it; the sun and all that reaches for it; the seasons and all that passes with them.

Throughout the history of America, the phrase "a place in the country" has been invested with multiple meanings. To some, it was any place not in "the city." As those cities grew and spread out, the country became a vague entity, amoeba-like in its constantly changing boundaries. It existed outside of the suburbs proper, preferably marked by dirt roads and a horse cart here and there. Then the suburbs burgeoned into edge cities, and The Country became capitalized. It now laid claim to roads that had mostly succumbed to a crust of blacktop and even a few stop signs. But the stray non-motorized buggy and rural free delivery still existed, lending credence to the notion of true Country.

Somewhere along the way, someone got the idea that The Country could be boxed up, and that little pieces of it could be bought and sold. A grapevine wreath entwined with sprigs of bittersweet and festooned with a gingham ribbon, a burlap pillow filled with balsam needles and potpourri, autumn leaves and milkweed seeds preserved in acrylic paperweights—these are all thoughtful gifts that we set on our windowsills and hang on our doors to remind us of where we really come from and to whence we hope to return.

It's no accident or fickle twist of fate that we have begun wanting to surround ourselves with the

There is something soothing and almost mystical about a trip down a country road. Most likely it's because these roads remind us that one's journey is often more important than one's destination.

PLATINO.

*T*he covered bridge has become a symbol of the pastoral ideal, embodying a time when bridges were more than simple spans across waterways. They were unofficial social centers, providing farmers who were driving herds from pasture to pasture with an excuse to stop and talk with one another about the weather and the latest livestock prices. Farm women passing on the way to and from town could visit under the bridge's sheltering shade and share the latest recipes and news from the marketplace, while their children played hide-and-seek among the foundation stones. How many young lovers held hands and kissed between these protective walls? Is it any wonder that one of the most moving love stories of the past decade—Robert James Waller's *The Bridges of Madison County*—revolved around these archetypal wooden "caves" whose presence spans the centuries between us and our ancestors?

*E*ven the simplest of covered bridges, humble, open-sided structures like this one, bespoke the care and craftsmanship that went into their making. Hand cut stone supports this wood-shingled trestle, under whose roof many country folks escaped sudden summer downpours, and on whose generous timbers many a truant schoolboy perched barefoot in late spring, dog sprawled beside him, jigging a cane pole for "sunnies."

trappings of The Country. These things embody the sense of connectedness we feel when we acknowledge our real home. Certainly, there are those among us who can no more envision the country as their home than they could imagine living on the moon. These people are examples of what science has called "adaptation." They have not merely learned to live with the realities of everyday life; they have evolved to such an extent that they no longer feel the tug of their primeval roots.

But the smell of wood smoke on an autumn breeze, the sight of spring's first robin, or the sound of a screech owl hooting in the night is enough to send many of us into a reverie of Country dreams.

What do we find so irresistible about rural living? What draws us away from the cores of society and far afield? I believe The Country provides an answer to a question that we all ask ourselves at one time or another: *Where do I belong?* The question stands just below *Why am I here?* on the hierarchy of importance in the ranks of universal inquiry, and it frequently dominates our thoughts from adolescence on. For some of us, finding its answer becomes an obsession.

We write about it. Ernest Hemingway needed only "a clean, well-lighted place," and Virginia Woolf yearned for "a room of one's own."

This covered bridge in Arkville, New York, also served as a community bulletin board for posters and handbills announcing upcoming events. In an era before graffiti defaced nearly every public space, the large and colorful posters—many advertising the pending arrival of traveling circuses and sideshows—offered visual excitement to eyes weary of bleached wood and dusty roads.

This view of a covered bridge in the western U.S. almost gives the traveler a sense of being about to pass through a portal that transports one from a tame and silent woodland to the wild, mountainous regions beyond. It might serve as a visual metaphor for that ambiguous place where the civilized turns into the wild, and the safety and assurance of city life gives way to the uncertainty of life on the land. Like all doors, it leads both ways.

We read about it. Few of us haven't enjoyed Norman McLean's *A River Runs Through It,* a memoir of his own inner search, which manifested itself in a passion for fly fishing.

Some of us go so far as to uproot ourselves and move physically in search of it. Consider the thousands who left their homelands and ventured in search of something better in a new land, then moved from the relative safety of our early cities and sold their worldly belongings in exchange for passage across the Great Plains by way of Conestoga wagon and a team of oxen. We seek to know where we stand in the broad scope of things, craving our niche in the universe. We long for a sense of place.

Many of us find this sense of place on a sojourn into The Country. For some of us, the feeling of belonging might come while walking a rural back road, or while making our way through a long-forgotten orchard strewn with fallen apples. For others, the revelation comes while sitting on the edge of a cold mountain brook or watching heat waves shimmer off the desert floor. For still others, it occurs while standing amidst a wheat field, listening to the rusty *c-r-e-a-k* of a windmill still pumping away for a family long since gone. We've never been here before, but somehow we know this place. It is ours, and it has always been ours. In the most profound sense, it is us, and we are it.

If knowledge is power, then self-knowledge is close to omnipotence. But this knowledge exacts a price that we cannot anticipate until the bill is paid. The same collective subconscious that responded to our inquiry requires an even exchange from us. Whenever we experience our own personal epiphany, the repayment begins. Some small echo, a remembered ache, brings us back to this place where, lives ago, we played as children, sweated under a blistering sun, broke the ground for the first time, lost a loved one. We know, and the land reminds us. It demands that we remember. And the memory, once manifest, never leaves. It haunts us through myriad details for the rest of our days.

That quiet voice is what makes us notice the shifting angle of the sun as it slides from the zenith of summer magnificence to its autumnal equinox. It is the pull at our hearts when we hear the geese honking overhead on their journey south to warmer lands. Memory is what makes us turn around and go back when we pass the tumbledown remains of an old farmstead, to search among the ruins of someone else's dreams for a fleeting insight into our own uncertain lives.

LIFE IN THE SLOW LANE

Celebrated architect Frank Lloyd Wright lamented a characteristic of the human animal that he called "the pig-piling instinct," the trait that makes us want to locate the centers of our everyday lives very close to others. It's true—we find safety in numbers and efficiency in shared resources. Humans are social creatures, and this instinct gave birth to the development of cities in the "Old World," the European

$\mathcal{P}$erhaps nothing is quite so evocative of a day in the country as the *clop-clop* of horses' hooves clattering upon the timbers of a covered bridge. A sunny day's ride in a surrey, with everyone dressed in their summer best--men in their straw boaters and women with parasols and mutton-chop sleeves--was a welcome diversion from the endless chores of the homestead. 🖋

One thing that lends a dirt road so much more personality than a paved one is its ability to record the passing of those who have traveled on it. The soft surface often holds wheel tracks, hoof marks, and footprints for all to see until the next heavy rain, when the "slate" is wiped clean, ready to receive the next traveler's signature. ❦

continent. Nevertheless, enforced gregariousness must have spurred resentment even then, for the French philosopher Jean-Jacques Rousseau referred to 18th-century cities as "the sink of the human race."

In America, most towns were born of similar social impulses, but their development into real cities arose out of a need for manufacturing efficiency. It's my notion that with citification came a peculiar development in the American psyche—a mindset often referred to as the "cowboy mentality."

Our nation was born of a need for independence from a heavy-handed monarchy. No longer were England's colonial subjects willing to be taxed to support a government in which they could not participate, to be ruled by laws that were either unjust or irrelevant to their new lives, or to see the fruits of their labors taken from them and shipped back to the mother country for distribution among the aristocracy. As Thomas Jefferson later wrote in a letter to a friend, "The mass of mankind has not been born with saddles on their backs, nor a favored few booted and spurred, ready to ride them legitimately, by the grace of God."

It was time for a change, and somewhere in the dimly lit back rooms of restless insurgents, the American Spirit sputtered to life with a cry that would rend the fabric of the most far-reaching empire ever known, one that would weave its dissident thread throughout history from that moment on. This spirit didn't die with the Revolutionary War and the attainment of American independence. Like all dynamic

This prosperous farmer's success is made obvious by his fine, large estate, by the presence of pleasure boats that imply leisure time, and by the waterfront location. Here, he waters his matched pair of mules at the river before moving a piece of machinery. His attire and hunting dog suggest that this gentleman has worked his way out of the fields, and may run his acreage from behind a polished, rolltop desk.

*T*his abandoned mill still stands as a reminder that men worked best when they worked with nature, not against it. Harnessing the energy of a river's flow made it possible for country folks to do everything from grinding corn and rolling oats to sawing logs into floorboards and wall planks. Ironically, the more comfortable folks became, the farther away from the earth they moved.

*Y*ou can almost hear the slow, wooden squeak of this water wheel as it turned tirelessly in service of the mill. It's hard not to wonder at the dedication of those who kept its spindle greased, replaced missing paddles, and cleared debris from its path after high water. At what point did the effort of maintaining the mill exceed its usefulness? When did hard work, patience, and perseverance finally yield to the onslaught of technology, trading a life of quiet toil for a career governed by schedules and accompanied by noisy, artificial power? These silent boards will keep that story to themselves. ❦

*F*alling Creek Mill near Hickory, North Carolina, stood proud when this photo was taken around the turn of the century. The large water wheel, intact spokes, paddles, and gears tell the story of a prosperous mill that probably succumbed to the pressures of electric and diesel-powered technology only after it had made its owner a tidy living as a water-powered "utility." ❦

Keystone View Company,
Manufacturers and Publishers.

Meadville, Pa. St. Louis, Mo.
Copyright 1900 by B. L. Singley.

689—A Sad Predicament

*C*ountry roads lead many places, but rare is the road that doesn't at some point branch off toward the local "swimmin' hole." Unfortunately for this astonished lad, others have arrived to share his enthusiasm for a day near the water, leaving him to cower behind the reeds "in the altogether," awaiting his chance to return to shore and retrieve his dignity along with his clothes ❦

ideas, it changed form and grew into the vision that compelled people to ford rivers, cross mountain ranges, and trek across a continent in search of freedom and the promise of opportunity that came to be known as the American Dream.

The penultimate American icon is the cowboy, a man alone by choice and capable of living off his wits and acquired skills, beholden to no one. This romantic ideal of a life without ties evolved into a more stationary but no less powerful being we call the farmer. The farmer punches no clocks, but lives in time with the seasons, doing things his own way and living or dying by the wisdom of his decisions. This direct descendant of the cowboy can't—or more likely won't—give in to

any "pig piling instincts" that might be rambling about in his subconscious, for he needs the solace of wide open spaces in which to live. He does not wish to participate in the artificial, removed–from–nature pursuits that a life in manufacturing requires. His offspring and their families have created the character of Rural America, which permeates our national life to this day.

Indeed, America's roots are in the soil. In 1800, fully 90 percent of the working population in the United States was engaged in agriculture. At the time of the country's bicentennial celebration in 1976, only about five percent worked on farms. Although each contemporary farm worker produced enough food to support over 20 people, a vast improvement over earlier production levels, these figures arguably indicate that most modern-day people are supplied with food for the body while being deprived of sustenance for the soul.

Before he became one of our nation's founding fathers, Thomas Jefferson was a Virginia farmer. He loved the feel and smell of the earth and the solitude offered by a rural life. An educated man with a poet's heart, Jefferson wryly observed that "the mobs of great cities add just so much to the support of pure government as sores do to the strength of the human body." He understood that success comes not just from the work of busy hands, but from the serenity of a quiet soul, and he—along with many others—believed that this serenity was a product of life outside the city.

With that in mind, let's head for country roads, for The Country begins along those byways. As we travel, we leave behind the manicured lawns held in check by paved curbs, and the scrappy, scrubby quack grass starts to meander carelessly across its proper boundaries onto the road's shoulder. The Country asserts itself more strongly as we reach a spot where roadside trees begin to outnumber billboards and neon signs, and we finally arrive in The Country proper when we turn off the main highway onto a road whose pavement has more cracks than solid spots, and whose mailboxes stand on posts at the end of private lanes.

If we stop, close our eyes, and relax for just a moment, it's not hard to imagine ourselves back in time, back in the heyday of Rural America.

The deep scores in this road, which seems as quaint and peaceful as a country road can be, tell the tale of a wagon that became mired in a post-rain mudhole. Notice, too, the increased road width before the grove of trees, where vehicles traveling in opposite directions could pull over to let one another pass. It's an example of neighborly consideration born of necessity.

Not much more than a cart path, this rugged byway carries us past two dirt farmers who are probably breaking first ground in the spring. This kind of ground breaking was the toughest, especially in areas where the soil had a high clay content. The plowshare had to overcome not only the sticky wetness of meltwater-saturated earth, but also the denseness of soil that had been packed down by winter snows for up to six months in northern zones. This could be the reason for using three horses instead of one, and for employing an extra plowhand to guide the reins while the other man simply tries to control the bucking plow itself. A second plowing was often necessary in order to till and sow.

*T*his scene of a farmer putting hay up into shocks could have been witnessed by a passerby during any season except winter. With each cutting, the sweetness and nutrient content of the hay diminished. The last bales, put up by the light of long, orange shafts of autumn sun, were but a pale reminder of the hearty, rich-smelling sheaves that first lined the boards of the empty haymow.

The end of the country road for many, these old tombstones bear silent testimony to the toll taken by a hard life working the land. Death was perhaps an easier notion to bear for folks like these, who lived close enough to nature to witness firsthand the inevitable cycles of life and death. Two hundred or more years old even when this photo was taken, Edward Gray's marker indicates how long people have been wresting a living from the earth in these parts. Their reward: a peaceful, perpetual slumber beneath the fragrant green grass, among singing birds and the whispering leaves of the trees. 🌿

SHADY LANE NEAR CLUB HOUSE,
MONTROSE, PA.

THE REXALL DRUG STORE
F. D. MORRIS & CO.
MONTROSE, PA.

CHAPTER 2

WORKING DAYS, FAMILY NIGHTS

Working Days, Family Nights

That the lives of Americans who lived in rural areas were rigorous and often difficult is common knowledge. Just what those lives consisted of may not be so well-known.

In a time when living simply was not only accepted but necessary, tasks were performed in a gender-segregated manner. Women generally did the domestic chores, while men cultivated and tilled the soil, harvested the crops, and cared for the livestock and equipment. I say "generally" because, although women were not usually considered physically strong enough to do heavy labor or intellectually capable of making big decisions, social conventions were bent at times when all able bodies or minds were needed. But for the most part, the house was the woman's domain; everything outside was the man's.

One can reflect on the apparent unfairness of this social arrangement from the perspective of either sex, but it was a system designed to get the work done. Any first-year psychology student is familiar with Maslow's Hierarchy of Needs, a theoretical scale of human survival requirements that begins with the basics of food, shelter, and clothing and graduates to desirable but not necessarily essential things such as love, praise, and entertainment. It is a widely accepted and logical theory.

According to Maslow's hierarchy, the early rural Americans were at base level, consumed by the reality of eking out a living from a harsh land that allowed little time for anything else. Debating the issue of male/ female equality would have required at least a post-secondary education and vocabulary sufficient to explore the problems posed by that issue. The conversations would have been lengthy and divisive, requiring a great deal of time and energy—just as they do now. Many of these people had barely finished the elementary grades. Not only that, but in the midst of striking out for unknown lands, settling a homestead, and running a farm, men and women had neither the time nor the energy for involved arguments.

"*B*e it ever so humble . . ." And it was. First introduced in North America by Swedish immigrants around 1640, the log cabin was rustic and functional. Here an elderly woman poses in front of her shake-roofed cabin. ❧

*I*t was a common practice for rural folks to pose with their homes, because for many, owning land and building a home was a dream achieved only through a lifetime of backbreaking work and sacrifice. In our nation's early years, it was not unusual for a person to die in the same house in which he or she was born. Although bare logs were eventually covered with clapboards or siding and roofs were redone using asphalt shingles instead of wooden shakes, homes built on newly settled land were often owned by the original families for generations. ❧

Therefore, most couples had a tacit agreement, given voice only in their marriage vows, to accept social conventions and get the job done. When you're hungry and cold, you don't argue about who will raise the food or make the clothes; the person who is best-suited and available does the task, and that was usually the person whose upbringing and socialization equipped him or her with the proper skills. It may seem severe, especially given the strides made in modern times, but in exchange for this quiet acquiescence to conventional mores, settlers laid claim to some things we can't begin to hope for in the present day.

Our forebears had an irrefutable sense of right and wrong, good and bad, acceptable and unacceptable. There were few moral gray areas to navigate and few unknown depths to plumb. Everyone knew what was expected of them, and no one had the brain-numbing task of constantly trying to reinvent themselves in response to the whims of a trend-obsessed society. Their minds were free to concentrate on the work at hand, and their solace was the knowledge that everyone's work was important and necessary.

Husband and wife were partners in every sense of the word; they knew the joy of truly sharing a life with each other, down to the bare bones of it. Her word, though often lacking the legal authority of her husband's, was law in the household. It was often as expressive in its silence as his most resounding shout.

This large hearth area, probably from a New England home, remains much the same as it might have appeared in Colonial times. The style of the hanging lantern, the long-handled fireplace implements, the iron kettles, and the spinning wheel— as well as the tableware displayed in the sideboard—indicate pre-Revolutionary life in America, when even the cities offered only rugged, labor-intensive living. However, the abundance of these items also indicates that the people who lived in this stone house with flagged floors enjoyed a fair amount of wealth.

The handiwork of an accomplished tinsmith—an ornate, punched-tin lantern, scoop, ladle, watering can, bowls, and numerous decorative items—is evident at this hearth. The hearth was the central area of every home before the invention of the cookstove, when kitchens became separate rooms. Note the hand-cranked coffee mill (upper right); a long-handled waffle iron (center); and the hand bellows (righthand corner, behind the warming bin). The wrought ironware in the picture at the right hangs neatly from the trammel. During actual food preparation, these implements would not be so well-organized. ❦

Their success as partners and farmers depended on their ability to read each other—to become intimately aware of each other's needs, desires, and skills. The sharing of labor fostered a tight bond that held at bay the trivial insecurities that plague so many in the late days of this twentieth century.

Just as the dynamics between marriage partners were immutable, so was the relationship between children and their parents. There was no calling one's parents by their first names; "sir" and "ma'am" were often the only acceptable forms of address. Anything less formal indicated an appalling lack of respect for

𝒯his 1903 photo indicates that the large cooking hearth remained viable and useful past the turn of the century for some rural homes. This one had already been around for a while, judging by the gaps between the firebrick on the floor, the patchwork in the tuckpointing behind the logs, and the scarring on the thick timber over the fireplace. ❧

A humble hearth graces this pioneer family cabin of square, rough-hewn timbers, below. Everything about this scene—the open tin lamp, the single stewpot, and the absence of brick flooring—suggests that the inhabitants lived a simple, rustic life. It's quite possible that the small kettle was used only to cook what was brought home in the game bag over the hearth; the finished meals were undoubtedly served on the plain pewter platter at the center. The only vestige of wealth evident here is the ornate candlestick in the middle of the mantel, most likely a family heirloom that served as a reminder of an easier life back in the East or in the Old Country. 🌿

Many a long, dark evening was brightened by the flames in the fireplace of this heavy-timbered home. You can almost smell the freshly baked bread that slid from the paddle at left as the cook prepared to serve hearty stew from the large cauldron. In Colonial New England, most homes were rather dark and dreary, because only the well-to-do could afford scarce glass for window-panes. Those who could had them fashioned after the Tudor style then popular in England, which utilized diamond-shaped panes set in strips of lead and then mounted in wood casements. If these windows opened at all, they opened out on hinges, not in the sliding manner that is common today. Many of these windows disappeared during the American Revolution, as the lead strips were melted down to make ammunition for the muskets of the Minutemen. 🌿

Some wealthy squire most likely built this Dutch Manor style house of fieldstone and mortar, to be used as a second home or "country estate" so he could escape the confines of a city such as New York or Philadelphia. These thick-walled structures were particularly comfortable, because their natural insulating properties kept the house cool in summer and warm in winter.

*C*haracterized by its ornate "gingerbread" woodwork and its decorative, lathe-turned spindles, this large house is a classic example of American Victorian style. Between 1850 and 1900, concurrent with most of the reign of England's Queen Victoria, America's northern states experienced rapid growth and a booming economy, and new architecture reflected that prosperity. In his book *American Houses,* Edwin Hoag writes, "They were days when people overdressed, studied books of etiquette, put on airs—and did the same with their houses." 🌿

one's elders, which simply was not tolerated. But the rules were not so much limitations as guidelines; children knew what was expected of them and grew within those boundaries to be respectful adults themselves.

This respect extended to other members of the immediate family, and to friends, neighbors, and even strangers. Grandparents, aunts, uncles, and cousins often lived together in the same house, or at least on the same property; the convocation of the generations provided role models for youngsters and a steady, constant framework of family and strength that all members could depend on and return to in times of shaken confidence. How many of us yearn for that reassurance today, but have nowhere to turn? It's no surprise that television shows like *The Waltons* were such long-running favorites. Many of us seek family unity and a sense of shared destiny, advantages enjoyed by rural families whose very lives depended on their ability to work and thrive together in their own little corner of America.

And so it was that a strong set of kindred roots was planted along with each successive crop, and was nurtured to fruition with each new harvest.

ALL IN A DAY'S WORK

If the farm wife reigned supreme over her domain, she was a queen who wielded her scepter with calloused hands. Her day began early, as she had to cook a hearty breakfast to sustain her family and the field workers until the noon meal. As farms grew larger, these workers often consisted of more than just her husband and their children, so the food was apt to be plentiful.

In very early times, before the availability of cookstoves, she had to prepare meals over an open fire in the hearth, which was a rather complicated affair.

*T*he imposing Victorian structure shown above bespeaks a prosperous rural family whose income probably no longer depended on the whims of nature, and whose inhabitants most likely had jobs "in town." Its shutters are drawn against a high afternoon sun, a procedure necessary to keep rooms cool in the days before air conditioning. 🌿

First she hauled wooden buckets of water from a nearby stream (or a well, if she was lucky), used to boil oatmeal, gruel, or corn mush, and to prepare coffee. She boiled the water over the open fire in kettles hung on a long iron rod, or trammel. The trammel was constructed so that it was affixed on one side to an upright pole, allowing the cook to swing it back and forth, over and off of the fire, in order to control the cooking temperature.

Baked goods were prepared in stoneware crockery and poured into tin pans for baking. Bread was kneaded by hand and allowed two risings before it was shaped into loaves and slid into the oven on a long-handled, wooden paddle. The bread oven was actually an opening built into the hearth side of the chimney, equipped with a small wooden door to hold the heat in. Another common way to bake involved using a Dutch oven—a cast iron kettle with three stubby legs and a heavy lid whose lip hung over the pot's edges by about an inch. Once filled with stew or casserole fixings, this pot was put directly into the fire, over some hot embers at the edge, and the lid was covered with more hot coals. The method distributed heat fairly evenly around the kettle, which resulted in more satisfactorily "done" dishes.

During summer and fall, fruits and vegetables were served fresh from the garden or orchard, entailing a great deal of hand preparation—washing, snapping, coring, peeling, and cutting—and after that, cooking if so desired. After the harvest, preserves were canned for use in cold weather months.

Beverages were usually limited to liquids that did not have to be kept cool for long, such as coffee, tea, water, and cider. Breakfast was the time for milk, since it was fresh from the morning's milking and was not in danger of spoiling. The cream was skimmed off and later churned into butter or poured over fresh berries or peaches. Bananas and citrus fruits were virtually unheard of outside the large cities, as they are fragile

*T*hese simple clapboard houses reflect the lives of families who have transcended the subsistence stage and are now able to spend some time in leisure activities. Obviously, these homeowners chose to put part of themselves into their surroundings by landscaping—adding personal touches such as trellises, bird baths, sidewalks, manicured shrubbery, and other decorative elements. During the Victorian era, the writings of romanticist John Ruskin and his peers encouraged people to rise above a survival level of thought into the realm of the aesthetic, thus giving rise to a culture of personal, creative expression among American homeowners. ❦

*N*othing provided more relaxation after a hard day in the fields than a quiet evening on the porch swing, listening to the song of the whippoorwill and watching the summer breeze sway the limbs of the oak in the front yard. And on a hot, summer Saturday, there was no better place to enjoy a cold glass of fresh lemonade. ❦

and perishable and could not withstand the time and rough handling involved in the over-the-road transportation of the era. Later, the invention of iceboxes and refrigerated rail cars made the storing and transport of perishable items possible.

Anyone who attempts to cook, even using today's methods, can appreciate the great skill of farm wives who prepared hearty meals that came together just when everyone was ready to eat. Their creative abilities make the phrase "domestic arts" more understandable.

After everyone was fed and off to work, the women of course had to do the dishes, a task that was accomplished by drawing more fresh water and heating it over the fire. While the water was heating, the farm wife might enjoy a bit of time to herself as she ate her own breakfast. Then the hot water was poured into stationary basins for washing and used sparingly for a rinse in a separate tub. Next, the dishes were dried— hopefully with the help of some of the children—and stacked on the sideboard (a kind of rough cabinet) until their next use.

If it was laundry day, she would tackle that job next. Washing had to be accomplished by the light of day, because it was an outdoor job. Imagine having to plan your laundry schedule by the weather. Again, much water was drawn. It was boiled in large iron cauldrons, which were suspended by chains from a tripod and positioned over an open fire. Early on, the clothes were dumped into this boiling cauldron and stirred with a large paddle or stick to loosen dirt from the fabric.

A no-nonsense midwestern farmhouse reflects the industriousness of its owner, as he heads to the barn for a late-morning milking. The man's attire and the spare, austere setting could be due to the effects of the Great Depression, during which this shot was taken. ❧

*A*ll gables, bay windows, and decorative woodwork, this farmhouse rambled and sprawled in order to accommodate its undoubtedly large family. The autos and the man's clothing suggest that the photo was taken in the late 1920s or early 1930s. ✺

washing out. The vat was tilted slightly to one end, where a hole or crevice allowed the runoff to escape into a bucket. The runoff was lye. It was heated in a cauldron with animal lard and stirred constantly to assure proper mixing and neutralization of the lye's alkalinity, which made the substance otherwise very poisonous. When properly mixed, it was poured into old tin pans or other containers to "set up," and subsequently cut into conveniently sized cakes. This soap had its own particular, not unpleasant smell. Perfumed varieties were not introduced until the Victorian era, when commercially milled soap began to appear.

Later, washboards were invented to facilitate scrubbing.

Suds were worked up by hand from a cake of hard, gritty, waxy-looking homemade soap. This soap was produced with lye, rendered by dripping water through old wood ashes that had been collected and stored from previous fires. The ashes were dumped into a makeshift vat—often no more than a hollowed-out log—which was lined with corn husks to prevent the ashes from

After several hours of washing, the clothes were hung out to dry on lines strung between trees or buildings. This was done even in cold weather. After the clothes had frozen stiff outside, they were taken down and thawed in the kitchen near the stove, and allowed to dry more completely before being ironed. This next step was begun by setting cast irons on stones near the fire in the hearth (or later, on top of the wood stove). The farm woman had several irons, so that one or more was heated while another was being used and, consequently, cooling off. The irons were grasped with a thick potholder or hotpad and pressed against the fabric on a long, padded board or on top of a flat surface such as the kitchen table.

By this time, the lunch hour was quickly arriving, and the women began putting together cold sandwiches and cakes. These were packed in baskets and taken along with jars or crocks of fresh, cold water (or later, when citrus fruit became available on the frontier, lemonade) to the men working in the fields. Then the wives would return and do housework—sewing, dusting, sweeping, milking, churning—until suppertime approached, when the meal preparation began again. Women with older children were lucky, because they had help with the chores and no longer had to attend to toddlers. Those with younger children often required the help of an aunt or grandmother to

Young people pose on the front porch of their Victorian home, complete with white picket fence. The many apparent additions and the age of these young men and women suggest that they are children who grew up in this house, either back for a visit or not quite "out of the nest" yet. ❦

supervise the children while they worked. If the farm wife did not have the company of other adults or older children, she was left to fend for herself, performing these tasks with an infant under one arm, on her lap, or close by in a cradle.

After the turn of the twentieth century, many began to recognize the housewife's job as the huge amount of work it was. Fortunately, many rural women had become literate enough to enjoy magazines such as *McClure's, Frank Leslie's Illustrated Weekly,* and *Life.* These publications serviced the needs of busy women whom advertisers were eager to reach with their ever-expanding lines of timesaving household products. Every so often, rural areas near universities were served by local publications that were put out by the

school's staff, or by articles that the faculty members wrote for regional magazines and newspapers.

Such was the case for farm wives living near the University of Wisconsin in the 1910s. Nellie Kedzie Jones, professor of home economics there (and previously the first woman professor at the Kansas State College of Agriculture), wrote a series of letters to a friend that were reprinted as columns in a Wisconsin publication called *The Country Gentleman*. Her letters shared many practical insights aimed at making rural life easier and less stressful for women, and her advice was eagerly anticipated in every issue between 1912 and 1916. In one of her columns, Nellie wrote:

Really the housewife's day begins yesterday though a man's day begins shortly before breakfast. That means you must do as much of the breakfast work as possible the night before. I would suggest, therefore, that plenty of good kindling and fine wood, seasoned wood, must be in the box before you are in bed.

Do not let two great big jobs land on you in the same day. Do not be caught so that you will have to bake on the same day that Ben has extra hired men on hand for you to cook for. He must let you know in time. Do not let your butter run low so that you must churn on wash day. Do not begin some hard job in the forenoon that will take far more time and strength than you had supposed, when guests are coming in the afternoon.

Ms. Jones also knew the value of not allowing chores to dominate the family's entire day. She advised sagely:

A batch of unbaked bread buried in the far corner of the garden may be a good investment. By that I mean, be ready to sacrifice the less for the greater. Ben may be suddenly called to town, and comes in and begs you to go with him just when your bread ought to go into the oven. Knead the bread down quickly, put it into a cold earthenware crock, cover and set it away in either the ice box or on the cellar bottom. Probably it will be all right to make into loaves when you get home, but if it is not, don't cry over spilled milk. You can make muffins if you have to.

Two or three hours together in the open air, measured in health, happiness, and mutual planning for farm and home, might have results worth many batches of bread. Some women are so busy with little things they do not recognize a big thing when it stares them in the face.

Don't hurry at your meals. You will have to hurry to get them, but eat them at leisure. I have been in farm homes where the meals were devoured in record time and all hands stampeded. I could think only of the well-filled trough, licked clean in a jiffy and deserted.

FROM SUN TO SUN

Rural men were no less tied to their daily duties, and their days were long indeed. Often up before the sun to attend to milking chores, the men and older boys

*A*n evolving record of the growth of its family, this cut-stone house includes several rear additions, and the bowed-out upper third of the chimney indicates a half-story loft addition, possibly for more bedrooms or storage. The bell on the roof may have been used to summon workers in from the fields at mealtime, or the house may have doubled as a community schoolhouse. ❧

Perhaps no other part of the homestead was as important or as often visited as the well. Tired, thirsty hands came in from the fields in the evening and gathered round it to gulp fresh, clear, stinging-cold water from an enamel ladle. They discussed the day's accomplishments and tomorrow's goals, and then washed up before heading to the main house for a hearty supper. It's not too far-fetched to liken these wells of yesteryear to today's office watercoolers. Both serve as community gathering places. ❦

swung their long john-clad legs off their beds and into a pair of baggy trousers or bib overalls. The bed, on its rope support and ticking mattress, groaned a little at the shifting of the weight, as if commenting on the cold winter morning. On went the woolen socks and the heavy-soled work boots, then it was down the stairs and out to the barn. The older boys fetched any wood or water still needed by Mama for her cooking, then headed out to help Papa.

A lantern lit the way to the barn, swinging slowly from side to side, and the

From a stereopticon slide humorously entitled "The Dinner Party," this image illustrates a common sight at just about any home outside of large cities—feeding time for the chickens. Because they are small and don't require a great deal of care, chickens were kept even by non-farmers. They supplied fresh eggs, an occasional dinner or picnic lunch, organic pest control, and the beauty of living lawn ornaments. 🌿

4165. The Dinner Party.

only sounds were a far-off hoot from a barred owl in the treeline and the crunch of boots on cold gravel. In the clear, still air, every noise carried and bounced off walls, trees, and posts. The barn door was swung open, releasing air redolent of hay, rolled oats, and just a bit of manure—not at all unpleasant in cool weather. The lantern was hung near the milking parlor, and the cows were led into their stalls. They munched contentedly on fresh hay as the farm men hitched them into their stanchions and pulled up milking stools. The boys and Papa took turns milking and feeding the other stock.

On very early homesteads, the stock might consist of only one or two cows for milk (and maybe beef), a hog, and a goat or a sheep. The animals were often housed in a small, lean-to building more like a shed than a barn. It wasn't until the farm was more well-established that large dairy barns such as the ones we see today were built.

Soon the air rung with the *ping, ping* of the milk streams hitting the sides of a metal bucket, playing a familiar little tune with an easy, regular beat. When the udders were empty and the pails full, the excess was emptied into lidded cans for later processing and stored

in the milk cellar, which remained cool in warm weather. During very hot weather when even the deepest fruit or milk cellar was invaded by warm air, milk cans were often set into the edges of fast-running streams to prevent spoilage.

Before heading back in to the table, Papa and the boys splashed their faces and washed their hands in a porcelain basin, towelling off with a sackcloth. Then everyone sat down to a hot, nourishing meal of fresh, plump eggs, homemade biscuits with fresh-churned

*I*n the early morning light, these rows must have looked long indeed to the people behind the plows, as they watched the land stretch clear to the horizon and beyond. Here a team of oxen pulls the breaking plow, which chews through the hard crust created by winter packing, melting, and stray roots. This allows the horse-drawn cultivating plow to follow behind, creating the furrows into which seed will be dropped. 🌿

butter and strawberry or grape preserves, smoke-cured ham or sausage, and fried potatoes. If they had the good fortune to be located near a stand of sugar maples, they might have some pancakes or waffles hot off the griddle and covered with syrup they had boiled down themselves. Sometimes oatmeal was served, with raisins and walnuts added for flavor.

After finishing their meals, the men headed out to the barn again, this time to collect the tools they would need for the day's work. In the winter, this consisted of fence mending, which often took the entire day or even an entire week if the farm was large. During the harvest season, when a feisty bull charged a fence or nature took its toll on a section, the men could only make emergency repairs, because the harvest wouldn't wait. But in winter, when the pastures were empty or seldom used, permanent, strong repairs could be performed, even if the weather wasn't ideal.

Harnesses, saddles, and other tack were also repaired, as were farm tools and machinery if the farm had any. Most products wore pretty well, which points out a significant difference between now and then. Then, products were manufactured with longevity in mind; they were made to be used, and many became

*G*randma pauses from her labors drawing water to savor a smoke from her corncob pipe. Notice the hand crank on the side of the wooden well cover, which made winching a full barrel of water to the surface much easier. Because they performed this kind of physical labor every day, most rural people were in prime physical shape without any need for health clubs or jogging. 🌿

At the end of the week, chores are done for a while, and it's time to pick up a few things in town and do some socializing. The heavy draft horse that pulls the plow is pressed into double duty as a carriage steed, and the small shay is off down the long dirt road. Its occupants are undoubtedly looking forward to a break from the isolation of the rural farm, and to a visit with neighbors and friends at the market. 🌾

more beautiful and functional with continued use. Now, things are made to be looked at. They may break if you actually try to use them, or at best they wear out quickly. The irony wouldn't be lost on those rural folks who wore the character into their tools.

Other household and farmyard problems often needed attention: broken seats in the outhouse; a stuck

or squeaky pump handle; dirty chimneys and broken mortar; a bent or broken weather vane that needed mending; windows that needed panes replaced. The list was virtually endless. By repairing and maintaining what they had won at such dear prices, country folks avoided waste and often practiced what we now call recycling. Tool handles were reused, cut, and shaped to fit the ax, hammer, or shovel head they would join. Cream and milk were put in metal cans and glass bottles, not throwaway paper cartons. Feed bags were made into towels, pillowcases, or children's clothing. Even food scraps were tossed to the hogs or composted, and no one congratulated themselves for their righteous behavior. Doing otherwise amounted to stupidity.

Winter was also the time for smoking and curing meats after the recent slaughter; rendering lard for use in soap and cooking, and for grease; going to auction for new stock; and taking care of the necessary paperwork and supply ordering that went undone during the busy season. Later, as spring approached, the maple sap began running, and it was time to tap the trees, collect the sap, and boil it down over the constantly watched fire. This was—and still is—a very time-

There is perhaps nothing more evocative of life on the farm than a barn with a haymow full of sweet-smelling golden bales. For rural families, the full mow also served as a symbol of security for the coming months. It was a reminder of their long days of field labor—an activity that reinforced family bonds as well as providing for basic needs. 🌿

*E*veryone enjoys a nice, cool dip in the river on a hot summer afternoon.

consuming task, even if a small number of trees were being tapped.

In spring the men delivered calves, lambs, and foals, and took care of plowing and planting. Seeds were ordered and sorted, and the fields were closely watched in order to determine just the right time for planting. Of course, one of the many almanacs was consulted when available, as were "the signs." All kinds of forecasts were made, based on animals, insects,

plants, weather, the planets, and even fire. It may seem strange to us that people would rely on such forecasts, but it's not so strange if you understand that their lives were lived very close to nature. They knew what they saw, and they believed what made sense to them— whatever seemed relevant and logical.

Once it was determined that plowing time had arrived, harnesses were checked again, oiled and fitted to that season's pulling animals. The original plowing

After a day of grazing in the pasture, these cattle head for the cool of the barn and a few scoops of oats. The slow rhythms of country living haven't changed much, and except for the primitive fence, this could be a scene from a modern-day farm. ✺

The birth of a calf has always been cause for excitement and wonder on the farm, and this little fellow seems surprised at his own arrival. But a thorough washing from his mother's tongue and a bed of soft straw has made his entry into the world a little easier to take, and he'll soon join the veterans of the barn in the farm's daily routine. ✺

animals were oxen, those stout, hardy animals that had survived the trip West to settlement. Later, mules or draft horses might replace them. Depending on where the farm was located, one or two plowings might be necessary. In areas of heavy rain or snowfall, the surface of the earth was packed so hard that one plowing was required just to break the hard crust, and a second one was needed to plow the furrows for planting. The time it took to complete the tilling and cultivating varied according to this situation and the size of the acreage to be planted.

After planting time, it was hurry up and wait until the seedlings rose, and then came the endless

A little girl spreads the joy of food among her flock of feathered friends in this 1904 stereopticon slide entitled "Breakfast Time." Although it's a cute sight, children were not simply decorative elements around the farm. They were a necessary part of the labor force required to run a successful enterprise, and they were trained in their duties as early as possible. ❦

*P*orky has found the oat bucket, and he's helping himself. It's up to these two brave young boys to separate the large, aggressive beast from the object of his desire. Judging by their expressions, it isn't a task they relish, but the chance for heroism doesn't come along every day for a rural boy, so they jump right in. 🌾

weeks and months of weeding, fertilizing, and removing pests from the plants. After the plants had grown sturdy, weeding was done by hand for long hours in the fields. At this time all able-bodied persons, women included, were out there pitching in to ensure the survival of the crop. Barring floods, severe wind, or hail, this never-ending labor resulted in a successful harvest.

AFTER THE SUN GOES DOWN

Although hard work was both respected and necessary, rural families knew that a life of uninterrupted drudgery was not good for the soul or the body, so they often attended to their entertainment with as much dedication as they went at the rest of their lives. After the last milking was done and the wood had been brought in for the next day's fire, it was time to settle in for a restful evening.

Before electricity, the farm truly operated at the pace of nature, with cycles of light and darkness limiting the activities of its occupants. On long summer evenings, the porch was a place to sit and enjoy the breeze while Mama or Papa and maybe a few farmhands lingered over coffee or told ghost stories. When the sun went down early in the cold months, only the most determined reader would attempt to pore over

*E*veryone gets into the act on the farm. Here Puss gets a little squirt as a reward for his imitation of a Kodiak bear. 🌿

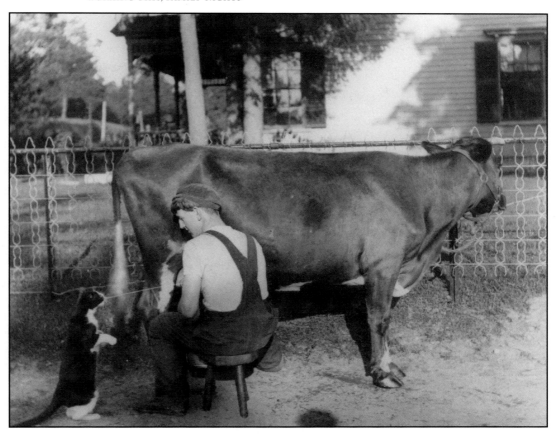

seed catalogs or magazines or the rare book. More often, Mama and Papa would take the time to sit together over a hot cup of coffee and share the day's experiences, discussing problems that had arisen or successes to be grateful for. They would plan the next day's schedule as the children sat playing quietly by the light of the fire or the heat of the woodstove.

Cat's cradle was a favorite game, played with string wound inventively between little fingers in predetermined patterns and passed back and forth between the players' hands. Children also played with things that their parents had made for them—rag dolls, small carved wooden figures, wagons, puppets, and toy horses. The checkerboard might be brought out for a match between the older children and Grandpa, while Grandma knitted quietly in the corner rocker, enjoying the presence of her family. Papa might be handy with a fiddle, banjo, or dulcimer, accompanied by Junior on the harmonica or jew's harp. Someone might even play the piano if the family was fortunate enough to have one. A bit of music and singing always brought a smile to weary faces.

Their proximity to the cycles of nature and the realities of life and death reinforced a strong religious

*M*ilking was a simple enough chore, so it often became one of the first to be tackled by youngsters. These boys seem to be enjoying their newfound responsibility. Their patient bovine friend seems a little wary of the inexperienced hands, but the second boy is apparently soothing her apprehensions. 🌱

faith in many rural families. Without the encumbrances of material wealth and social ambitions, theirs was a simple existence to which the words of the Bible spoke clearly and understandably. Often, families spent at least part of their evenings reading from the Bible, which served not only as inspiration for their faith, but also as reading lessons for the youngsters.

Sundays were held sacred as days of rest, which often included visits to neighboring farms after church services in the morning. These visits made up the bulk of rural social life, with the exception of church suppers, ice cream socials, and an occasional school play. Although such social occasions were not numerous, they were important reminders of the sense of community that held together the rural way of life. 〰️

The harvest was a "make or break" time for those who lived off of their land. If the tilling and planting went well and the crop had a chance to grow to maturity, all that was necessary for a successful year was getting it out of the fields and into storage or off to market. However, this was not always an easy task. Even modern-day prognosticators with fancy scientific equipment are often fooled by the will of Mother Nature.

Early farmers, whose very lives depended on their ability to get the crops in before heavy rain or snow arrived, were even less informed. It's no wonder, then, that they depended heavily on common sense and previous experience to decide when it was time to begin the harvest. But a little folklore sure couldn't hurt, and they welcomed all the help they could get.

General weather predictions involved temperatures and precipitation or lack of it. These were the two elements that dictated planting and harvesting activities. A few forecasting tips are listed here:

Rain is to be expected if:
- leaves turn backside up.
- cows lie down in the pasture.
- there is a ring around the moon. (Count the number of stars in the ring. Rain will come within that same number of days.)
- the sun sets among clouds.
- an ant covers the entrance to his anthill.
- chimney smoke drifts to the ground.
- birds fly low.

Here's more rain lore:
- If it begins to rain on the day of the full moon, it will continue raining until the moon quarters.
- If it has been a while since it rained, and the rain begins before 7 a.m., it will stop before 11 a.m.

- If it rains on "Blasting Days" (the three longest days of the year), mast such as chestnuts and acorns will be scarce for hogs and wildlife to feed on that year.

Fair weather can be expected if:
- A screech owl calls.
- Smoke rises.
- Crickets chirp (the temperature will also rise).

Part of what the farmer had to decide was how much of each crop to sell at market and how much to keep for his own use. If he expected a short, easy winter, he might take more hay and grain to market for a bigger cash income, knowing his stock animals could be put out to pasture from time to time. But if the winter was expected to be severe, he would have to hold back more for their consumption, diminishing his cash intake for the year. For a small operation with a very slight margin of error, this decision could be critical. Knowing when to get the barn ready for long-term animal inhabitation due to lack of open pasture was also necessary. So although forecasting the winter is a dubious practice at best, it was important. Superstitions naturally developed around this endeavor, and many of them are still believed today. Here are some of the more interesting beliefs:

- The number of days old that the moon is at first snow indicates the number of snowfalls that will occur during the winter.
- If it's cloudy and smoke rises, there's a chance of snow.
- When you build a fire outside and it pops, it will snow in three days.
- Two frosts and a lot of rain mean cold weather will come soon.
- A late frost indicates a bad winter ahead.

- Every frost or fog in August will be matched with a snowy winter day.
- At least three severe fogs in June or July mean early snow.
- If the first snow stays for three days, another will come on top of it.
- The hotter the summer, the colder the winter.

The behavior and appearance of plants, animals, and insects also foretold the severity of the coming winter, according to folk beliefs. Bad winters were portended by:

- Squirrels gathering nuts early, beginning in mid to late September.
- Muskrats building large lodges.
- Birds eating all the berries early.
- Juncoes feeding in the trees instead of on the ground.
- Wild hogs gathering bedding materials.
- Thicker-than-usual fur on the bottom of rabbits' feet.
- Squirrels growing bushier tails.
- Blackberry bushes blooming heavily.
- Carrots growing deeper than usual.
- Onions growing more layers.
- Bark growing thickly on trees.
- Grapes and apples maturing early.
- Bees and hornets building nests closer to the ground than usual.
- Worms bending upward.
- Crickets singing in the chimney.
- Ants building higher anthills.
- A thick black band around the woolly bear caterpillar (the thicker the band, the worse the winter).
- The woolly bear appearing before the first frost.

*T*he never-ending chore of milking was often undertaken outside the barn, so both the cow and the milker could enjoy a bit of sunshine and nice weather. 🌿

"*C*'mon, just a little higher and you'll be able to reach the latch!" This horse seems to be coaching his perky little companion. Rural animals often became fast friends in their shared duties, extending the farm family beyond the walls of the main house. 🌿

The smile on this young woman's face makes her appear as happy as her contented charge to be filling the pail with warm, foamy milk. Perhaps she's imagining the fresh butter she'll churn from it, or how good a cold glass will taste with a slab of the fresh cherry pie that's cooling on the windowsill. ❧

The idyllic farm scene depicted in this stereopticon slide is perhaps idealized, as the young woman seems too perfectly coiffed and too tidily dressed to have washed the laundry that's hanging in the background before moving on to milking. Laundry was a dirty and grueling task that most certainly would have loosened a few strands from her "Gibson Girl" hairdo and left a few smudges on her full-length gingham frock. ❧

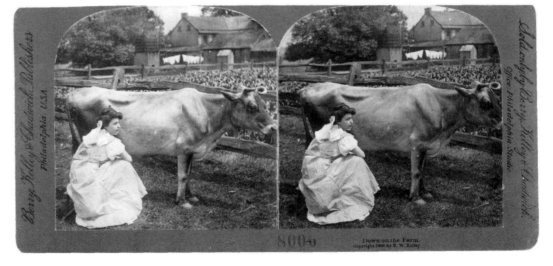

*E*veryone needs to relax from time to time, and this little burro is making good use of a vacant hammock to recover from the recent rigors of birth. ❦

*O*ne can only guess how this stereopticon slide was captioned, but we can infer from the young woman's earnest expression and her bouquet of wildflowers that she harbors great fondness for her porcine partner, who was apparently waiting at the window for her arrival. ❦

*T*his motley crew of mousers-in-training holds still for a rare portrait of feline felicity. No doubt they were off immediately following this portrait to demonstrate their worth as productive members of the farmstead by chasing butterflies, birds, and any other creature that threatened the farm's tranquility. ❦

*E*ven the meager prosperity of a farming family was often shared, if grudgingly, with hoboes who passed through looking for work during the Great Depression. Usually, the itinerant men would exchange field work for a good meal and a place to sleep before moving on. This kind of country hospitality kept many a decent man who was down on his luck from starving or freezing to death during those dark days of our country's history. ❧

*I*f a man and his wife were lucky enough to avoid wearing out their bodies by toiling in the fields and the kitchen, advanced age in a rural setting was a pleasure. It offered the chance to sit back and enjoy simple activities and quiet conversation in soothing surroundings. ❧

CHAPTER 3

WHEN THE WORK WAS DONE

WHEN THE WORK WAS DONE

*F*ree time for the country dweller was almost nonexistent in the very early years of settlement, because nearly every waking hour was spent toiling to provide sustenance for the body in some way—food, shelter, or clothing. But people, being the way they are, have always found some way to indulge in the pastimes that define the difference between merely existing and really living—things like travel, music, mirth, and the company of other human souls.

As the years passed, newfangled inventions provided the hardworking farmer and his family with labor-saving devices, which in turn gave them more free hours in their long days. Depending on the family's beliefs and the degree of religious fervor, time not spent on chores and school might be devoted to anything from the quiet sobriety of Bible studies and prayer to the raucous frivolity of a square dance or a medicine show.

Often the choice of leisure activities depended largely on the gender of those involved. In the 1800s, the Christian church played a large part in the lives of women, both rural and urban. Charitable church projects were among the few activities outside of the home that were considered worthy of a proper, feminine woman; they were among the even *fewer* activities that young, unmarried women and girls could engage in without a chaperone—especially during the morally restrictive Victorian era. In 1830, French writer Frances Trollope observed about America that "there is no other country in the world where religion makes so large a part of the amusement and occupation of the ladies."

These women organized fund-raising events such as quilting bees, box socials (where each young woman prepared a hearty lunch and packed it in a fancy box to be bid on by eligible young men), auctions, and musical recitals, the proceeds of which were donated to the church or used as financial relief for the local poor. In an era before social welfare programs existed, these events supplied not only much-needed charity for victims of poverty, but also a socially acceptable means

The "horseless carriage" made its rather inauspicious debut late in the nineteenth century; by 1895, only four of these vehicles were on the road in the entire country. Rolling along on rubber tires—at first tubeless—the early electric or gas-powered machines were noisy and slow. They were unreliable, and unable to negotiate steep grades or carry heavy loads like a team of mules or horses. As a result, the occupants of passing wagons often laughed them off with a cry of, "Get a horse!" 🌿

$\mathcal{P}$otatoes, melons, and cabbage were all cash crops raised to be traded in town or sold at market for money, which was then used to buy things that couldn't be traded for. These produce runs often accounted for the bulk of family trips to town. Generally, only a few family members accompanied the mounds of fruits and vegetables that took up most of the room in the wagon or, as shown here, the truck bed. This kind of "truck farming" was responsible for the subsistence of many rural families during the Great Depression of the "Dirty Thirties," so named for the peculiarly common dust storms that arose from the parched, cracked, and largely fruitless fields of the Great Plains region. 🌱

through which young people could meet and begin to practice the rituals of courtship.

Activities such as these, which we might today view as stodgy and limiting, actually provided a welcome structure for what must have been, as it is now, a confusing and frightening time in the development of young men and women. This seems especially relevant because serious courtship commonly began at a very early age—17 or 18 for boys, and as early as 14 for girls.

On the other end of the spectrum, the typically male pursuits of hunting, fishing, playing checkers and cards, and gambling often filled the leisure evenings and weekends of men who didn't attend church services or support the related volunteer events. As is the case today, a favorite activity of the nineteenth-century homeowner was puttering about the house, enjoying the fruits of his many labors, performing odd jobs, or pursuing hobbies such as carving or furniture-making. And as always, children who weren't working could be found playing games, daydreaming, or—if they were from a better-educated family—reading. Whatever the age or gender, one thing held true for the residents of Rural America: They played as hard as they worked.

Like their modern counterparts, early rural families craved changes of scenery. The change might involve just a walk to the neighbor's farm, or a real trip to town. The birth of a new baby, a wedding, a barn-raising, or a canning party were all legitimate excuses for packing up a carpetbag with a few changes of clothing and filling a picnic basket with nourishment.

$\mathcal{E}$arly on, the main mode of transportation for a family or large group was a practical if not very comfortable wagon, or "carryall." The one shown here is not much more than a produce cart loaded with corn shocks for a ride from the field to the main house. For a longer trip to town or a visit to a neighboring farm, a larger, buckboard-style wagon was used. True buckboards had one or several bench-like seats facing forward and mounted on flexible softwood boards, affording a measure of shock-absorbing comfort. A less comfortable pile of straw served as the seat for most travelers—usually flattened and not very soft after a few trips. Later models had more sophisticated wheels than those shown here, which were most likely fashioned from a cross-section of a tree found on the farmer's property. This type of slab wheel was structurally weak, due to natural cross-grain and lack of reinforcement. It was replaced by wheels fashioned by professional coopers and wheelwrights, featuring spokes radiating out from a hub on a greased axle bearing, and treaded with a smooth metal rim for long, even wear. After the early days of settlement, oxen were forsaken for mules, which were more versatile and easier to care for. The mules were a cross between a horse and a donkey, and were the animal of choice for wagon pulling. 🌿

For an extended visit, the family piled into a large buckboard or buggy. Short visits could be made by sleigh in the winter, but the high degree of maintenance required by livestock during cold weather made longer trips impossible. Even during warm weather, if someone could not be found to perform the feeding and milking, someone (usually Father) had to stay behind.

Trips into town were the most common junkets made by rural families, and these were much anticipated by everyone. Later on, day trips were made in newfangled automobiles at breathtaking speeds of 15 m.p.h. or more, but for most of the century, travel was undertaken at the easy pace of a pair of mules pulling a wagon loaded with Ma, Pa, and the kids.

FRIENDS ON THE WAY

The sights encountered on the way to town were often as exciting as the destination itself. The rural family might pass by a roadside tavern or an inn that

Laying Corner Stone
M E Church, Aug, 26.
Copyright 1908.
by Lee L Zuver, Tionesta, Pa.

Because the church was an integral part of most rural communities, it's no surprise that an event such as the laying of the cornerstone for a new chapel building would draw the kind of crowd this one did in 1908 at Tionesta, Pennsylvania. For the happy occasion, everyone turned out in their Sunday best: the men in their celluloid collars, vests, bow ties and black frock coats; the women in broad-brimmed, flower-festooned hats, modest, floor-length skirts (no bustles or mutton chop sleeves for these unassuming country women) and modified "Gibson Girl" hairdos. 🌾

The House of the Lord was a humble abode in early America, as it remains to this day in many rural communities. The congregation that worshipped in this small frame building had the wherewithal to purchase a bell and construct a spartan and unadorned steeple, but could not, apparently, afford a separate parsonage. The rough, unfinished addition on the back of the church probably housed the pastor of the small flock of faithful followers. It's likely that the preacher also served as groundskeeper, undertaker, and all-around maintenance man. Despite its humble appearance, this little church doubtless took its place at the center of many community events, and left its front doors unlocked to the weary traveler, the out-of-town visitor, or any wayward soul who sought shelter and—if the pastor was lucky—spiritual guidance. 🌿

adorned its walls with a beautiful panorama of exotic colors and images created by a traveling painter. If family members chose to stop and inspect the work, they might be talked into scheduling a painted family portrait by the same artist. He would later visit their farm and complete the painting for as low as $3 to $5 per head—or as high as $25 per person, if he could persuade the customer of its value and knew the family could afford such an exorbitant fee. If the artist was particularly dextrous, he might bring along a sharp pair of scissors and cut the children's silhouettes out of crisp black paper for 50 cents apiece. Most of these itinerant artists were put out of business after the 1840s, due to the rise in popularity of photography.

Moving along the road, our traveling family might encounter a peddler, his brightly painted wagon hung with shiny pots and pans that clanged against the wooden sides, announcing his approach. The peddler would size them up from a distance as a family that had cash on hand—they were headed toward town with no produce to sell, so they must be prepared to buy. If he persuaded them to stop for a while, they would be treated to a full show of his many wares. With a flourish exhibited only by the most practiced showmen, he would produce goods intended to make Mother's eyes sparkle: shiny pins, needles, and other sewing notions, fancy fabrics and buttons, French collars to adorn a smart new dress, satin capes, and intricate lace. If that weren't enough, he would display a vast array of such extravagances as silver spoons, combs, brooches, and bracelets, all the while gauging Mother's reaction to his presentation.

Farm auctions have always attracted thrifty farmers, professional bargain hunters, and folks who were just downright curious. The collection of "runabouts" here indicates a fairly prosperous crowd. With a body shape greatly resembling the yet-to-be-introduced Ford Model T automobile, these little buggies were introduced in the mid-1850s. By the 1890s, they were being offered in the Sears Roebuck catalog at a price of $425 for the top-of-the-line model. These vehicles sported such luxuries as upholstered leather seats and convertible leather tops. 🌾

𝒜 trip to the feed mill was a regular part of any farmer's schedule, especially if his own fields were devoted to cash crops instead of livestock fodder. The kindly-looking man pictured here might have grown up in the business, learning the trade at his father's knee and now passing it on to his own children. ❧

Of course, he was a man of health as well as wealth, all due to his plentiful stock of patent medicines, including the castor oil so dreaded by children everywhere and smelling salts. The latter were *de riguer* for any home prosperous enough to have a parlor, where frank conversation might often cause a proper lady to swoon.

Then the peddler's swift-moving hands would produce baskets, tin, and woodenware to tempt Mother with the prospect of greater ease in the kitchen and enhanced visual appeal at the table. Aware of the great anticipation of the children, the peddler would move to the back of the wagon, from which he would withdraw songbooks, playing cards, baby toys, rattles, writing slates, whistles, dolls, balls, and spinning tops. As the children hovered longingly over the brightly colored objects, the peddler would sense Father's growing restlessness. Quickly, he would pull Father aside and show him an impressive cupboard stacked with boxes of shot and powder, fine cigars, and maybe a pack of "naughty" playing cards printed with girlie poses that wouldn't turn a head today.

Having thus hooked the entire family, the peddler would make a few well-placed comments to seal the sale and convince Father to part with a bit of the hard-earned cash that was originally meant for purchasing a bit of rope or some other piece of hardware that could wait until the next trip.

A problem might arise with the actual exchange of currency, for in the first half of the nineteenth century, no standard currency existed. Russian kopecks, Dutch rijksdollars, French and English specie, and Mexican and South American silver coins were all in circulation throughout the country. Some dubious financial

*A*nother image from the Dust Bowl era, this photo shows a tired mother and her daughter resting on a stoop in front of a store window. The fabric of their dresses still shows bright designs free of faded, patched, or threadbare spots, and although the girl's shoes exhibit wear, with the soles letting go on both feet, at least she *has* shoes, which were often considered a luxury during warm weather. We can only guess what's in the bag next to Mother, or what they're waiting for. Perhaps Brother is inside picking out a new hair comb, or maybe they're biding time while a friendly neighbor finishes shopping before giving them a lift home in his truck. 🌾

institutions, referred to as "wildcats" after the beasts that roamed the mountainous back regions where these institutions were often located, issued paper notes drawn on private banks. Because currency was issued without regulation, this paper money was often unsecured with anything of value, and was therefore nearly worthless outside the geographic region where it was issued. This problem was solved only after 1861, when banking became federally regulated and a standard national currency was issued.

After finalizing whatever deals were made, the family members packed their booty into the wagon and once again went on their way.

They might pass friends and acquaintances who were also enjoying a day away from home. Mother might hail a lone woman on horseback whose saddlebags were bulging with bundles of cloth, salves, and medicines. This respected woman, a midwife, would wave back, and again the wagon would pull over for a brief chat. Only five medical schools had been

*W*hen's the last time you saw apples at 25¢ for half a bushel? Today, you couldn't even get the empty basket for such a price. Pure maple syrup retails here for $2.75 a gallon, and honey is sold by the tin can. 🌿

established in the country by 1810, so rural families felt an acute shortage of trained doctors. They relied heavily on midwives, who not only delivered babies, but also provided a wide array of traditional homeopathic treatments, herbal remedies, and a smattering of medical practices to pull patients through everything from head colds to the measles. The only training a midwife received was her experience, often gained at the foot of a mother, aunt, or grandmother who also practiced the healing arts.

Because her knowledge was better than ignorance in a land that often wreaked physical havoc on its inhabitants, and because her cures often worked, the midwife was a highly regarded and appreciated member of rural society. She was one of the few women who could travel alone without having her virtue questioned, and her opinions were taken as seriously as those of men on many subjects. She stayed in the homes of her patients while they were being treated, and their hospitality was partial payment for her services. Her professional travels took her across an area that was often several counties wide, and her news of friends and neighbors was greatly cherished by farmbound wives whose social lives left much to be desired.

After catching up on the gossip about newly born humans and livestock—the former of interest to the women, the latter to the men—and other news of interest, the traveling family would bid the midwife farewell. Father would cluck the team back into action,

and they were soon rolling toward town once again.

As they approached the outskirts of town, they might pass the churchyard and wave to the sexton, who was tending the gravesites in the adjacent cemetery. The sexton served year-round as undertaker and bell-ringer; in winter, he might double as the snow warden for that stretch of road, meaning that he was responsible for keeping the road's snow cover flat and evenly packed, so sleighs could travel easily over it.

*T*itled "Circus Day in Goldfield, Nevada, 1907," this photo shows the entire town turned out for the sound and spectacle of one of the great traveling circuses, whose arrival was much ballyhooed by the front men who rode ahead to ensure good attendance. These advance men plastered huge, brightly colored posters (or broadsides) on every available flat space, and the advertisements showcased all the main attractions of the center ring: lion tamers, bareback riders, trapeze artists, the huge, exotic elephants, tigers, and dancing dogs. The aggressive public relations campaign served to work up such a frenzy, especially among children, that by the time the first wagons rolled into town, everyone was there to line Main Street. Ornately carved and painted wooden wagons, pulled by matched teams of fancy white or Arabian horses, carried the band, which thumped out merry tunes. These were followed by pony carts, trains of elephants, cage wagons containing wild animals, and others carrying the calliope and costumed riders. The parade of circus performers was its own best advertisement, and this "live media event" virtually guaranteed a packed tent every night the show was in town. How much farther removed from their often drab, workaday world could farm families get than sitting in a brightly lit tent filled with creatures from halfway across the globe, scantily-clad performers, and the smell of hot, buttered popcorn? 🌾

ARE WE THERE YET?

Once in town, Father would lead the mules to one of several watering troughs placed conveniently in front of the wooden sidewalks and tie them to a hitching post. There the animals would drink to cool off and would rest contentedly while the family went about its business. Father would help Mother and the girls down from their wagon perches, and the boys would jump over the sideboards into the dust of the street.

After deciding when and where to meet, they would often split up and head in separate directions, each with their own agenda to accomplish before going back home. Father most likely had some banking business to take care of, as well as a trip to the hardware store and a stop in the town saloon for a quick drink and some friendly banter. Mother might want to trade some eggs at the market for a bag of refined sugar or coffee beans, then pay a visit to the dress shop. The children would of course want to haunt the candy counter at the general store, relishing the feel of the cool glass as they pressed their noses against it while making long and anguished decisions about which penny candy to buy with the nickels that Pa had provided.

While waiting in line at the bank, Father might decide to treat himself to the services of the bootblack, whose practiced hands deftly applied polish and buffed his good leather shoes to a high shine. Later, he would admire them as they rested on the long brass rail that

*A*nother event that was a welcome distraction from the normally quiet rural life was the fair. State, regional, and county fairs filled a particularly large niche in the world of farm families, just as they do today. This institution originally came about as a way for those involved in agriculture to share their knowledge of a still-young science. But because entire families attended the events, they soon became opportunities for everyone to get involved. Children showed off their budding skills in animal care and husbandry; mothers participated in contests pitting their favorite food recipes against those of neighbors near and far; and fathers entered their favorite draft animals in friendly competition against their peers in weight-pulling contests. Of course, enterprising entrepreneurs and inventors recognized this gathering of like-minded people as the ideal opportunity to market their new products: home canning tools and supplies, farming equipment, labor-saving devices, and the requisite food and drink stands. While their parents were busy with this multitude of diversions, the children managed to keep themselves occupied by attending the numerous sideshows where the hucksters would call them into their mysterious tents to gawk in mildly horrified fascination at the cruelties of nature personified: the Bearded Lady, the Fat Man, the Two-Headed Boy. Before regulation of these kinds of activity, some unscrupulous characters were known to purposely inflict harm on children or other helpless individuals—such as putting a child in an odd-shaped vase until its body took on that shape permanently—for the sole purpose of making money from exhibiting them at such shows. However, for the most part these shows provided the only reliable source of income these unfortunate people could depend on, as an unenlightened society otherwise shunned them. ❦

Gaily festooned with pennants, flags, and multi-colored bunting, the livestock judging barn was arguably the liveliest place to be found at any fair. It was here that a year's worth of intense care, training, and money competed with similar efforts whenever cattle, horses, sheep, or pigs were brought into the ring. Reputations and fortunes were sometimes made and lost according to the judges' decisions—hence the intense concentration displayed by many of the viewers surrounding the fence in this photograph, which was taken in Louisville, Kentucky. ❧

ran along the bottom of the bar, and would be sure to protect them from stray streams of tobacco juice that might miss the spittoon in the corner.

Mother might run into a friend at the dress shop who had come to give the seamstress some business. Perhaps her husband had parlayed their small farm into more cash crops than livestock feed acreage, so she could now afford to hire the woman to do some of her sewing. Ready-made clothes didn't become available until the 1840s, and housewives prior to that time had two choices—learn to sew, or hire someone to do it. Around 1820, a woman might have paid about $3.95 for the two-and-a-half yards of woolen fabric needed to make a coat, fifty cents for 14 gold-gilt coat buttons, and $1.50 for the labor to put it together, making a grand total of $5.95—not a bad price for a nice birthday gift for her husband or child.

The children would pore over the candy case long and hard, nickels clenched in their sweaty little fists, before deciding to spend their money on large chunks of fudge, peanut brittle, popcorn balls, taffy, or gumdrops. The store might also display tantalizing glass jars full of licorice twists (black and red), dark chocolate non-pareils, wintergreen lozenges, jujubes, red hots, lollipops, and multi-colored jawbreakers. After an interminable time, the hand-heated coins would be exchanged for the winning choices, which were transferred from glass containers to a brown paper bag. Children would accept the prize, grasping it hard

around its soon-to-be-twisted top, and run into the street to look for school chums to tease and share with.

Soon Mother and Father would emerge from their respective establishments and gather up the children, and the family would once again board the wagon for the return trip, happy and tired from their busy afternoon. After getting back on the road, Mother would pull the jug of lemonade out from its burlap cover under the seat, where it had been hidden along with the picnic basket from the sun's heat, and pour some into a tin cup. The cup would be passed around with the sandwiches and pieces of cake to make the trip more enjoyable. Junior would not be too hungry after gorging himself on lemon drops, so he might not finish his sandwich before the rhythmic sway of the wagon rocked him off to sleep.

The rest of the children would then lay back in the bed of straw that covered the hard wagon boards, daydreaming or drifting off to sleep as the sun began to set and the fireflies started to twinkle against the blue mist that was forming over the river. The wagon wheels would clatter over the bridge and Mother would softly hum a hymn from last week's service as Father reined the team into the barnyard. After carrying the sleeping children in to their beds, Father would head back out to unhitch and curry the team and hang up the tack. Mother would tuck her babies in for the night, brush their cheeks with a kiss, and wish them all sweet dreams.✐

The photo offers a bird's-eye view of a typical midway, this one also from the Louisville State Fair. Clothing styles indicate that the shot was taken around the turn of the century, as does the presence of early automobiles. If you removed these elements, this could be a recent photo with all the requisite trappings—game tents, souvenir vendors, mechanized carnival rides, an agricultural building, a racetrack and, of course, Coca-Cola stands.

*H*ere's a sight you won't see anymore! Safety regulations for humans and welfare laws for the humane treatment of animals preclude a carnival act like this one today, but early traveling road shows often included such dangerous stunts. This horse and rider are jumping off a high platform into a shallow pool of water. The stunt was usually performed safely, due to the physics of water displacement and other factors, but the feat was nonetheless a risky one. It's obvious that the horse didn't participate in the act willingly—as evidenced by the man on top of the wooden tower, who slapped the animal's rear end to induce it to jump.

CHAPTER 4

A GALLERY OF THOSE WHO TILLED AND TOILED

A Gallery of Those Who Tilled and Toiled

Anyone who cares to look closely enough discovers that a person's face and body serve as a record of who they are, where they've been, and what they've done. Accomplishment sparkles in the eyes and adds to the erectness of one's carriage. Defeat bows the back, slows the step, and dulls the color of the skin. Loss manifests itself in a faraway look to the eyes, a droop at the corners of the mouth, and hands that are often restless. A sense of humor is betrayed by laugh lines around the eyes and mouth; worry etches deep lines into the brow and causes a tendency to clench the jaw and fidget.

The faces in this chapter tell their own stories. However long or short were the lives that sculpted these faces and bodies, one thing is for certain: they were lives connected to the soil, the sky, and the other lives around them. The years have worn some of the faces away and carved creases into others. Endless days of watching the sky for rain, keeping track of the stock, and wrenching a living from the earth have bent the backs of many, and the loss of hope for an easier life is present in the vacuum of more than a few eyes.

In the best of years, rural life was not easy; it could be merciless in the worst times. Disease often ravaged small communities or farms that were isolated from qualified medical care, to such an extent that no family was left unscathed by death's wide-swinging sickle. Elisabeth Spach Olson, a first-generation American and the child of immigrant parents, was born in Illinois on the midwestern frontier. In her memoir, *As I Remember It,* she writes in a voice that could only come from one accustomed to random and relentless loss:

Diphtheria was a dread disease and was always present and in some years would be in epidemic form. We had lost our little Alfred with it the year I was born. There was a sort of shanty house across the road from us, and the family living there lost three children one winter with diphtheria; a girl of 12, a boy 7 and a small one. The father died some time later, and the mother was left with three young boys and two girls.

This woman understood equality of the sexes in a way not fathomed by many today. In a world where the seasons won't wait, every able body was pressed into service, and every person in the family benefited from these labors.

Another family, the Reinhardts, lost their baby. It died of convulsions and Mrs. Reinhardt came to borrow pennies to put on the dead baby's eyes. In convulsions, the eyes rolled back and stayed open unless they were held in place with something—usually a penny. The next day Mother and I went over to see the family, and she showed us the little baby wrapped up in a blanket.

We might like to wax nostalgic about "the good old days," but anyone who lived through them would quickly let us know that many things about those days were anything but good. The following photographs serve as a tribute to those who dared venture into the unknown, using their wits and skills to help them build a life for themselves and their loved ones. Knowing there were no guarantees and no safeguards, these

courageous souls strode forth into the challenge of the future and, with the strength of their commitment, built the framework of our past.

Of all the crops raised by American farmers, tobacco is perhaps the most demanding. Not a hardy plant, tobacco is susceptible to attack by a host of insects, frost, and other weather damage. The backbreaking process of picking and drying the leaves on home-built racks made it one of the most despised crops, raised only for its cash value on the open market. In early America, the cash was desperately needed to buy the things that farmers couldn't trade for: farm implements, processed foods, medical care, and later, automobiles. It has been poignantly noted in such rural narratives as Ben Logan's *The Land Remembers* that farms growing only tobacco didn't last long. The crop took a heavy toll on the soil and on the people who raised it. 🌿

*O*ne thing that seems universal among photos of early Americans who made a living off the land is the look of bone-deep weariness on their faces and in their very demeanors. The slack posture, loosely hanging garments, and sunken, often haunted eyes belie their pride in surviving close to the earth. ❦

*T*here's no telling what this elderly lady is musing over as she puffs away on her corncob pipe. She might be laughing to herself about the fact that we all seem to want to collect things she would just as soon have thrown away: the chipped porcelain basins, her slatted wooden bucket, and that hard-to-clean spatterware bowl! ❦

*T*he house might be plain and her clothing simple, but a farm woman tried her best to add a little beauty and a bit of herself to her home, often through good baking and a few plants set on the windowsill. More often than not, these plants were herbs and spices commonly used fresh in cooking and valued for their medicinal and decorative qualities. 🌿

*O*nly the jauntily cocked corduroy cap belies the serious growl cast at the camera by this grizzled tiller of the soil. The sun and wind have bleached this man's face until he's as weathered as barnwood with the paint worn away, and the face that emerges from the top of his rough, homespun shirt might be made of the same fabric. ❧

A pause in the day's chores allows time for a portrait of this thoughtful, overall-clad granger. Unlike more "citified" gentlemen who glared forthrightly into the camera, farmers tended to look past the lens, uncomfortable with such outright scrutiny of their quiet, unassuming lives. This one seems impatient to get back to his familiar work routine and then on to a hot supper. ❧

*T*his portrait of a hardworking, humble old laborer conveys his gratitude for and appreciation of the simple things best exemplified by a life in Rural America. ❧

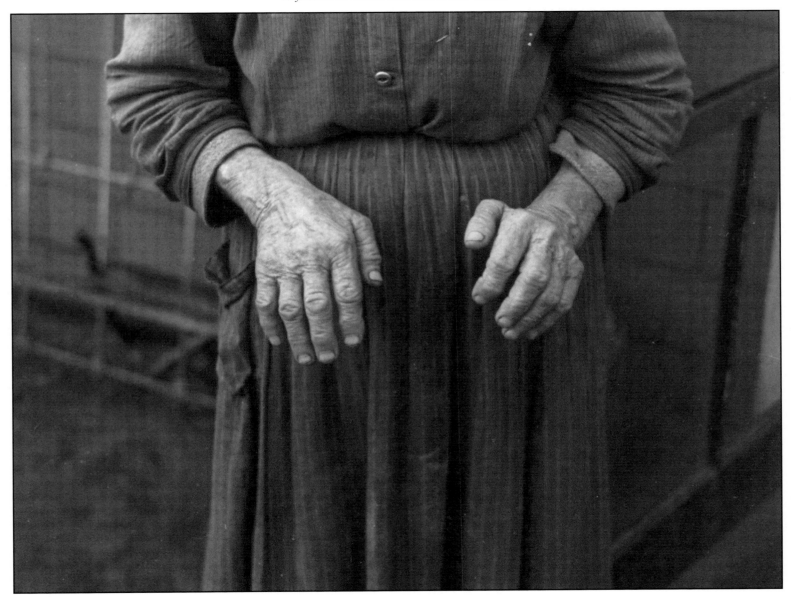

It's evening. The day's work is done, and it's time to head back along the split rail fence to wash up for dinner under the hand pump or at the well. The farmer's stooped posture gives away his fatigue.

*T*his early twentieth-century farmer finds humor and entertainment in one of the most repetitive and mundane tasks of his life—milking. His two cats are rewarded for their dedicated work as mousers by a few well-placed squirts from Bossy's udder. ❧

Keeping "varmints" out of the melon patch sometimes required more persuasive powers than the scarecrow could muster. This situation allows Grandpa to prove he hasn't lost his skill with a shotgun.

In this scene of domestic tranquility, Mother (or Grandma) sews while a child reads her lessons, accompanied by the family pet. Clean milk cans lie on the bench in preparation for tomorrow's milking, and the fire tripod and wooden buckets stand ready for laundry day. The size of the dwelling and the real glass windowpanes indicate a relatively prosperous homestead—as do the matching chairs and the well-dressed people. The ability of the girl to read also suggests that the family had the financial wherewithal to send her to school. ❧

A lengthy chore such as butter churning built both the muscles and the mind when the churner used the chance to catch up on a little reading. The little kitten also seizes an opportunity to lap up some splashed cream while its mistress is distracted. 🌿

A pair of old friends have a smoke and do a little whittling on the fencerow, since even a hardworking farmer needs a rest now and then. Perhaps they are recalling particularly good crop years, the tornado that ripped through the area a few years back, or the big snow of '88. Or maybe they're swapping stories about the incredible feats of some of their friends and neighbors.

Chapter 5

Children of The Land

CHILDREN OF THE LAND

*F*or the offspring of those who were driven to find their life's blood among the straight furrows of moist, black earth, work began at a young age and lasted a lifetime. Their lessons were learned as often from the stable or a seat on the fence post as from a schoolbook or a chalkboard. They may have lacked comfort and luxury, but they gained a thorough grounding in reality, balance, and a sense of the interconnectedness of all things living and inanimate. Consequently, they understood their place in the family, on the farm, in the community, and as a citizen of the world in ways that can be taught only through the eloquence of simple living.

Children were brought into the world not just because they were desired, but also because they were needed, and they derived from this a sense of purpose and innate value. The health of the human condition requires a certain sense of belonging, of being productive and necessary—a sense that today's world often fails to provide. These qualities promote a sense of responsibility and commitment that our modern society also fails to reliably cultivate. Perhaps our global awareness today causes us to feel disconnected from our fellow humans and the other species with whom we share the planet. In a world where one's physical horizons stretched wide but safely bounded the known world, one could develop a sense of oneself in concrete, definable, and visible terms.

If you were supposed to fetch firewood and didn't, the whole family suffered. Failure to follow directions for planting might mean little or no crop, a problem that would not be evident until it was too late to correct the error. A broken fence left unmended might result in the loss of a draft animal, which in turn could eliminate the entire family's ability to get around or perform chores. Every action or inaction had a direct and measurable consequence, and a child was bound to feel the effects of this equation in a very personal way.

At the same time, childhood was a time to be a child—not a fashion plate, not a miniature adult, not a

*A*s busy as they were, country parents were aware of their children's need for fun and stimulation. The more creative among them came up with unique ways of entertaining their youngsters. This lucky little girl was given a toddler-sized cart equipped with a modified harness to accommodate a pair of turkeys. Traveling photographers would also provide such props to entice parents into springing for a child's portrait. ❧

This cumbersome, heavy, wrought iron walker was more fancy than practical, in that it required a great deal more physical strength to operate than today's plastic and aluminum models. However, the infant in the photo appears undaunted by the task of propelling the unwieldy walker across the splintery floorboards in his bare feet. 🌿

Pride in craftsmanship is apparent in this early wicker perambulator (or "pram"). The ornate weaving patterns in the basket, combined with the solid, cast iron construction of the frame and wheels, is typical of a time when manufacturers built their products to last for generations.🌿

"*O*h, yeah? I've got a bigger splinter than *that,* right here in my toe!" A couple of ragamuffin farm girls use an overturned oil drum as a seat while exploring the dangers of running around barefoot. 🌱

*E*ven very young farm children became adept at finding the many hiding places employed by cagey hens that were trying to conceal their eggs. In fact, it became a game to try and outwit the wily creatures and find the eggs before they froze in the winter or spoiled in hot weather. 🌱

mathematical genius or a musical prodigy—just a child. It was a time for discovery of oneself, of others, of family ties, of the way things work, of life and death. Play was rambunctious, healthy, and fun. Toys were most often homemade, and operating them required the use of the brain as well as the dexterity of a child's limbs and digits. Most of all, play required the use of the imagination, an unknown quantity in much of today's childhood activity. Without television, and often without radio or movies, children turned to the fertile grounds of their own inventive minds. Very commonly, they even helped make their own playthings. Elisabeth Olson remembers:

The winters in those years—the 1890s—seemed to have much more snow than these later years. Father and the boys made sleds in the blacksmith shop, and they all got skates as soon as they were old enough. One day when the snows were too deep for my short feet, the boys hauled me to school on the sled. Evenings the older kids would get a farm boy whose parents had a bobsled and team of horses to drive, and they would pick up a group of friends and drive up and down the roads, singing songs, stop off at someone's house for coffee and sandwiches, and everybody had a good time. Sometimes they would gather at the river when the ice was thick and strong enough and have skating parties and lunch around a bonfire. Or they would gather on a hillside for a sliding party on moonlit nights. Winter was beautiful then.

In warmer weather, the children played games that still amuse youngsters today—blind man's bluff, tag, hide and seek. They played on homemade swings made from rope and boards and hung in trees; floated little wooden or paper boats in creeks and streams; held foot races and baseball games; and climbed trees. Family pets proved not only friendly but useful when smaller children were in need of a creature to pull their wagons or to play "cow" in a game of rodeo, in which Rover would gracefully if not happily acquiesce to being "roped" by the lariat of some aspiring young cowboy.

Whatever their games and pastimes, children then, as always, were not only playing but preparing for their lives as adults by learning to share and get along with others. They were rehearsing for the time to come, when they would take their places as productive citizens among their friends and families along the narrow, winding dirt roads of rural America.

*I*n early Country, feeding the horses was a favorite chore of farm children. The same holds true today.

A little boy, visiting his grandpa in the country for a few days and free to do the things that boys do, frolics freely with some ducks near the pond. ❧

Two pretty young girls, probably sisters, pose in a daisy field with a friendly pooch. This double image of domestic tranquility was viewed through a stereopticon—a sort of primitive "Viewmaster" that offered the illusion of three-dimensionality. Admiring the slides was a popular pastime in the parlors of the well-to-do. ❧

Children seem to have a natural affinity for animals, and the age-old bond between a little girl and her horse is illustrated by this photo of the pigtailed miss feeding her forelocked friend with oats held in her checkered gingham apron. This natural bond was strengthened by the close cooperation between farm families and their animals. Plowing, threshing, and any other job that required pulling proved the worth of any horse, mule, or ox that could haul the weight. Day in and day out, the slow rhythm of milking reinforced the necessary intimacy between human and dairy cow. And of course, there were the family pets—dogs and cats that pulled their own weight by herding sheep and cattle, and by keeping the outbuildings free of vermin. 🌿

This aproned farm girl doesn't seem to understand that Porky would rather make a pig of himself than act like a proper gentleman and use a spoon. 🌿

"TIRED HAYMAKERS."

PHOTO AND PUBL.
BY C.E. BROWN
HIGHLAND, N.Y.

*T*hese boys and girls stretch out in the field after a long morning of hayraking. Their "Sunday best" clothes and neatly combed hair indicate that they were posing for the camera of a traveling photographer. Nevertheless, if the farm was to remain viable, very young children were needed in the fields to till and sow, often using implements far larger than they were. ❦

"*A* daisy field, a collie dog and thee . . ." Everyone, including the youngest child and the family pooch, found a way to escape to the fragrant spring fields, where they could enjoy the return of the sun after a long, isolated winter on the farm. ❧

*I*tinerant photographers often rolled up in their darkroom wagons to stop at country homes and "make pictures" of family members who could not often get to town. Children were frequently photographed standing next to livestock or sitting on a small pony supplied by the photographer. ❧

"*P*laying house" is a little girl's pastime with a long and venerated history, but the tools of the trade have evolved over the years. This aspiring housewife from the turn of the century (opposite) practices laundering clothes with a miniature washboard and a wooden tub that's fitted with a little hand wringer. Her toys are replicas of the full-sized versions used by her mother. Emulation of adult activities is a natural learning process for young people, but it's uncertain whether any amount of child's play could have prepared this girl for the life of intense and unending labor that would face her as a farm wife. ❧

Even when the "Old West" wasn't yet so old, playing cowboys was a favorite game among American boys. If those boys just happened to have a couple of sturdy mules to help them ford the river in search of "dogies," so much the better. These upstate New York boys cross the Valkill River on their noble steeds, in a reenactment that still goes on today. ❦

An age-old dilemma faces this young brother and sister—what to do once the family food supply has become a family pet. The little girl declines to take the axe to the neck of her red-combed, strutting friend, who has followed her around the farmyard and kept her company for months while everyone else was too busy for her. Such unpleasant realities confronted all children who grew up in self-sufficient country families that raised grain, vegetables, herbs, and livestock, and had to process it all for use as food. Without supermarkets to depend upon, getting emotionally attached to the livestock was a luxury they could not allow themselves. ❦

A rather bare schoolhouse interior nevertheless indicates an above-average community investment, with real wood floors as opposed to the more common packed dirt, and plank ceilings instead of sod or thatch. The school also boasts actual desks instead of church pews (some communities couldn't afford a separate school), and a chapbook available for every child instead of just one for the schoolmaster.

The original caption for this photo reads, "Miss Blanche Lamont with her school at Heola, Montana, Oct. 1893." Miss Lamont's charges included at least 29 children and two dogs, which she undertook to educate in the discipline of the "Three Rs" in her roughly built, one-room schoolhouse. Teachers in rural communities often came from Eastern cities such as New York and Philadelphia, heading west after graduation for the promise of better wages and a freer life. 🖋

A far cry from the cramped cabins and dugout schoolhouses of the West, this whitewashed clapboard structure had real glass, shutters, and a bell tower. The building indicates that North Branch, New York, was a fairly wealthy and well-established community by 1883. This was probably the latest of several incarnations of the school building, as the area had been settled for well over a hundred years by the time this photograph was taken. 🌿

The hayride, still a favorite autumn activity, was also a popular pastime when there was no motorized alternative to horse-drawn vehicles. 🌿

Decorating the Maypole with flowers and garlands was a yearly ritual that marked the arrival of spring. Young girls dressed in frilly white frocks danced about the pole in the country schoolyard, singing songs to celebrate the end of the long prairie winter. 🌿

Chapter 6

The Harvest

THE HARVEST

After the work of planting, weeding, and caring for the crops all spring and summer, the light changed, and the sun began to set a bit earlier. The "dog days" of August had passed, and every once in a while the night carried a slight chill on its breeze. The whippoorwills chirped their syncopated, up-and-down song at regular intervals deep into the night, and the constant, unbroken trill of the katydids replaced the chirruping of night frogs. Days dawned on patches of goldenrod, suspended from which were large monarch cocoons. One morning Papa would return from an early walk in the fields, where he had examined the stalks of corn, the long stems of wheat, and the other crops, and announce that it was time. The harvest would begin.

From that moment on, the homestead roused itself from the languor of summer and kicked into high gear. Hired hands came by to occupy guest rooms for the duration. Mama, Grandma, and the girls spent most of their time in the kitchen when they weren't helping in the fields, and the horses and mules sprang out of their hot weather lethargy and into the work for which their breeding had equipped them. Once again, tack was cleaned and inspected, blades were sharpened on scythes and mowers, wagon wheels were put back into round and re-rimmed in the blacksmith shop, and the draft animals were shod.

From the moment there was enough light to see by until the last twilight ray illuminated the yard, everyone became cogs in a well-tuned machine designed to dig and gather, cut and stack, pile, tie, and move. Hay and straw were cut and baled by rows of scythe-wielding men, their muscles bulging and rippling under thin cotton shirts as the sweat poured off their constantly kinetic bodies. The scythes moved in an easy rhythm, their handles worn smooth by years of contact with calloused hands, the wood made strong by the oils absorbed from hard-working skin. *Swish, swish,* hissed their crescent-shaped blades, leaving half-moon swaths in their wake. Behind them, workers gathered the cut grass into sheaves or shocks, bundling and tying them

After mowing and piling, the hay or alfalfa was left to dry in the sunshine, then forked onto flat wagons to be transported back to the barn for final drying and storage. During this process, farmers had to be keenly aware of the weather, for a misreading of the clouds could spell disaster. If it looked like rain, hay already cut was quickly gathered and taken back to the shelter of the barn, for wet stuff was almost certain to rot, mildew, and spoil. The hay still standing in the fields was safe, because it could sway in the wind and dry out before cutting.

ALFALFA.

*H*eading to the fields with their long scythes, these men cut wheat or hay by hand, literally earning their bread by the sweat of their brows. This kind of direct connection between work and life fostered a sound work ethic that kept—and still keeps—farmers close to the land. 🌾

for loading onto a wagon. Later on, this was all done by machines, initially horse-drawn and then steam-powered.

Day after day, acre after acre of pungent plants was brought in. Everyone worked against time and the weather, especially if the crop was a late-maturing one. The longer a farmer waited to begin harvesting, the greater the chance that the harvest would be cut short or ruined by rain, or even snow. More than one nervous eye was cast constantly skyward when heavy, leaden clouds appeared on the horizon and thunder rolled ominously in the distance. On rainy days, all of the farm folks fervently hoped that the precipitation wouldn't last too long or amount to too much. Mucky fields were difficult to work in, and a saturated crop was nearly always destined to rot in fields or mildew in storage.

Only when the last bale was safely put up in the loft, the last of the potatoes, carrots, and apples were stored in bins of sawdust in the cool, dark cellar, and the jars of preserves were stacked neatly on shelves like so many colored bulbs did everyone relax and slow down. Then the hired men were paid off and sent on their way with some fresh-baked apple pie and a bottle of cider, and the pumpkins were brought in and stored where they were safe from the frost.

*H*and threshing, cutting, and gathering was as slow
and daunting a task as it appears, and the amount of
acreage a farmer could work was limited by the number
of people available to help him sow and harvest his crops.
This was the main reason farm families were so large;
the farmer and his wife created their own, unpaid labor
force by having children. ❦

*T*hese mule-drawn reapers, which allowed the operators
to work sitting down, were less physically demanding and
more efficient than hand-scything. They made longer (and
more productive) workdays possible, because exhaustion
didn't set in as early. ❦

After that, stubble was turned under and winter wheat was planted while the ground was still soft. Equipment was cleaned and oiled, the harnesses were polished and hung back in the barn, and mealtimes became more regular and leisurely. As the first flakes of snow began to fall, all the creatures on and around the farm settled into the pattern of the long winter's sleep, resting and replenishing themselves for the next cycle of life.

So went the seasons in Rural America, when we measured time by the length of shadows cast and not by consulting the eerily glowing faces of digital clocks; when we valued material goods for their usefulness and not because they enhanced our image; when we judged people by their character and not their clothes. Is it folly to wonder what those people whose faces appear in this book would think of us now? Perhaps not; it may be our salvation to wonder about such things, for it is only by considering their values that we might really investigate our own. Perhaps it is only in the backward view through the telescope of time that we will discover and truly recognize our own sense of place.

𝒜s is still done today, the fresh-cut hay was put up in windrows—long rows of short piles—to dry in the sun before being put up in the barn. Although this robbed the long grasses of some of their nutritional value, it also prevented premature spoilage during storage. To make sure the horses and cattle got as much nutrition as possible, they were allowed to graze right up until the first snowfall made pasture grass inaccessible.

*T*his wagon, below, is loaded and ready for the oxen to pull it back to the barn, where its precious golden cargo will be forked into a waiting haymow for use as winter feed and bedding for livestock that can no longer make it into the snow-laden pastures. ❧

A huge, soft pile of hay, above, makes a comfortable perch for this farm woman, who accompanies her family on the ride back from the field to the barn. Her mother has undoubtedly prepared a hearty supper of beef roast from the last season's slaughter, vegetables from the family's garden, and mounds of mashed potatoes and thick gravy. These plate-fillers were accompanied by loaves of warm, fresh bread or buttermilk biscuits straight from the oven, slathered with hand-churned sweet cream butter and preserves made from last summer's berry crop. For dessert, there was apple pie baked fresh from the bounty of the back orchard. ❧

This photo, circa 1915, shows the intensive labor required to harvest potatoes. This kind of work provided (and still provides) jobs for many itinerant laborers, making the farming sector a vital part of America's economy. ❧

This "threshing bee" was a familiar scene on many farms in early rural America, when neighbors understood that they had a responsibility to each other. At harvest time, farmers in a community often got together with their equipment and moved from farm to farm, until everyone's crops had been harvested and safely stored for the long winter or for later sale at market. These "bees" lasted for days at a time. Women and younger children also got together to prepare and serve food for the hungry laborers, a huge task that required many hours each day. 🌾

In this 1908 photo, men cut and bind corn shocks by hand. After drying in the fields, these shocks would be used as pig fodder, bedding material for barn stalls, and—in a bad year—as feed supplement for the cows and horses. 🌾

Thanks to such creative thinkers as Cyrus McCormick and John Appleby, reaping and binding became more automated and efficient tasks, which greatly increased the productivity of struggling farmers. Here, a hand-fed twine binder is run by the power of a diesel engine tractor, producing the convenient, stackable, and space-efficient square bales that we still see today. 🌿

*H*ere a man uses a primitive masher to reduce freshly picked apples to hearty sauce for canning. The runoff juice was collected and used to make cider for the women and children and a bit of "hard cider" or "applejack," which fermented into a tangy liquor. The menfolk enjoyed a drink after dinner when the harvest had been brought in and the early setting of the winter sun made the evenings long and ripe for storytelling. 🌿

PRESERVING

$\mathcal{J}$ust as men had their "threshing bees," women got together for "canning bees," where fruit, vegetables, and meat were cleaned, prepared, and canned in jars for high-pressure boiling, which preserved the great quantities of food that couldn't be consumed immediately. One wonders whether the lone gentleman at center was supervising or simply waiting around to steal a taste of the good things to come. 🌿

*T*his hillside scene presents a typical harvest image of corn shocks and pumpkins left in the wake of the harvest wagon. The harvesters would return later, taking it all back to the farmyard.

𝒯his woman gathers dried field corn, which will be stored in a wire crib for use as winter cattle, horse, and pig feed. She may also reserve a few ears for her colorful bird friends. ❧

16023. Gathering in the pumpkins in the Yakima Valley, Wash.

Young field hands in Washington's Yakima Valley haul pumpkins almost as large as themselves to the waiting wagon, which will haul the produce back to the farmyard for sorting and weighing before the pumpkins are taken to market. From there, they will be transported to processing plants and canned for the ubiquitous pumpkin pies that are served as part of the nation's Thanksgiving celebration. The late-fall day of gratitude was designated a legal holiday by Abraham Lincoln during the Civil War, some 40 years before this photograph was taken. ❦